The Business Of Bespoke

Pawan & Ashish Ishwar

CONTENTS

INTRODUCTION

When we came to Dubai from London in 2010 to start our own bespoke tailoring house, we had lots of knowledge about craftsmanship and bespoke tradition, which was missing in Dubai. We knew we were in the right place because Dubai and U.A.E, in general, did not have enough history and heritage as far as bespoke craftsmanship for suits was concerned. We also knew that we would be the only Savile Row trained tailors in the entire Gulf region, which got us very excited to start.

Once we started, we soon realized that we had all the knowledge as far as the craft was concerned but lacked the business acumen to run a successful tailoring house. We knew there was an outstanding balance between being a craftsman and being a successful businessman, and giving them both equal weights was not very easy. This was because being a tailor was a profession, and owning a tailoring house was a business. You did not want to be seen as merely a business person as then your craft loses credibility, and you did not want to be just a good craftsman as your business would suffer without sufficient profits and revenues to sustain.

While running Knights & Lords, our bespoke tailoring house, we had the right experiences at the right time, which made us learn from our mistakes and correct them quickly. We also stumbled upon opportunities that made us develop strategies that placed Knights & Lords among the most successful and respected tailoring houses in the region. We were fortunate enough to have these experiences and opportunities. Still, there are many craftsmen, businessmen, and start-ups who are not able to do a successful business simply because they only focus on the craftsmanship side of their enterprise and are not able to recognize opportunities that can help them to develop and implement strategies to become successful.

In this book, we have put down our entire journey of starting and running Knights & Lords along with our experiences, mistakes, opportunities, strategies, and, more importantly, all our trade secrets for everyone to read and learn from.

This is certainly not a guide to success as we recognize every single artisan, craftsman, or business person has a different journey, but what this book reveals are the strategies that we put in place and made us successful. If you are a craftsman, artisan, or business person who has some form of personalization or customization in the product or service you sell, this book will help you to implement these unique strategies which made Knights & Lords successful. It may or may not work in the same way for you. Still, it will certainly make your business better and give you a competitive edge over others, offering a similar custom product or service, resulting in a high customer retention rate.

Implementing these same strategies will give you different quantitative results than it gave us as every business is different, but the results will make your business grow organically with minimum expenditure in marketing and will eventually result in a good balance between having a strong and respected brand presence along with a financially successful business, a balance which is otherwise difficult to attain with professions that are focused on personalization, customization, and craftsmanship.

Success is not a destination, it is a journey, and we wish you the very best on making your journey a successful one as we have and continue to make ours.

WHY GET
INTO
THE BUSINESS OF
BESPOKE?

*"Entrepreneurial leadership requires
the ability to move quickly when the
opportunity presents itself."
- Brian Tracy*

The beauty of bespoke business is that there are many ways in which you can be unique and set yourself apart from any other industry as everything you do is personalized and made specially for your client keeping his individual characteristics in mind. This arrangement has many benefits which are listed below:

It is very lucrative and profitable: This is the first and most important thing in any business. As an entrepreneur, starting a business only makes sense if it is profitable. The profitability in this business comes from the fact that you do not need to invest and maintain inventory. What you make is completely on-demand, made only when the client places an order for it as it is especially made for them. The cost is further reduced by not being invested and maintaining an inventory, and you are also able to command higher margins because it is custom-made as per the specifications of your client. These two things put together gives you higher profitability compared to other industries.

Easier customer retention: Since you are treating your clients as individuals and not as mere number by crafting things that are aligned with their individual personality and lifestyle, they are more likely to remember you and return to you if they are satisfied as opposed to other industries which are more price sensitive and clients can only be retained by offering better prices than competitors.

Easier to position yourself as an authority: Any business that deals with a personalized or customized product or service is seen as a creative field where you are either a craftsman or an artisan or are a creative force behind a team of craftsmen or artisans. Depending on how you creatively express yourself with your creations, you are able to easily position yourself as an authority in your field of work by garnering the right media attention over and above other industries as you are not seen just as an average trader or business person but as someone who is unique and creative.

Once you have decided to start your own bespoke business, the next step is to focus on the thing that will ensure its success which is how your brand is perceived by your clients. This does not just require a simple strategy, it requires a brand image that projects your success through a unique brand story.

ESTABLISHING THE STORY

*"A great brand is a story that
never stops unfolding."*
-Tony Hsieh

Whether you are a bespoke tailor yourself, a craftsman, or just the founder of a custom clothing business, the first step is establishing the story behind your brand. Your brand story is what will make your potential clients connect with you once you have mentioned it personally or across the media and will be responsible for making them choose you as their custom clothier over and above others.

Your brand story must cover the following three key areas:

Your background

What is the one thing that made you decide that you need to start your own custom clothing business?

What is the motive behind it, and what you wish to accomplish with it?

While it is important to cover these three key areas in your brand story, it is more important to cover them in the right manner that will create a differentiation point for your brand compared to the others in the market.

Your Background

Information about your background should not just include why you are qualified to be their custom clothier but also showcase your credentials in a manner that creates a sense of trust in the eyes of the potential client who is getting this information personally or through media. This is always done by giving them a brief glimpse of your journey right from your humble beginnings to where you are today. This subconsciously tells the observer that you are trustworthy since you have included details of your struggles and details on how you worked your way up to get to where you are now. Human beings also inherently have a primitive instinct to value and respect something that is achieved with struggle, so mentioning your struggle will ignite a sense of respect for you in the eyes of the observer.

When we started our bespoke tailoring house in Dubai, our background was mentioned as follows:

Knights & Lords, a bespoke tailoring house in Dubai, is born out of the passion of Ashish & Pawan, two brothers who have been trained in Savile Row-London, the spiritual home of bespoke tailors. Ashish was a trouser under-cutter, and Pawan was a button-hole maker when they started as an apprentice on Savile Row. Ashish spent seven years, and Pawan spent five years to work their way up on to the cutting board and master the legendary 'Drape Cut' method of suit making.

As can be seen above, the fact that we have been trained in Savile Row, which is even today considered the beacon of bespoke clothing, showcases our qualifications and credentials in a manner that tells people that they can trust us to make their custom garments. It also briefly mentions how we started as an apprentice doing a much smaller tailoring job and how we struggled with years of work to become a cutter and mastered what is considered a coveted cut called the 'Drape Cut.' This will ensure that they respect the fact that mastering our craft has not come easy to us and respect us for providing our experience and expertise to them.

The background information certainly differs from person to person and business to business due to its individualistic nature. The important part to include in your background information is what qualifies you to become their custom clothier in a manner that makes them trust you and some brief information on your struggle towards getting to where you are today. Be sure to make it as brief and as concise as possible while covering these aspects because this is just one key area of your brand story, and the other two key areas are remaining to add to this to complete it.

What is the one thing that made you decide that you need to start your own custom clothing business?

Your background has already given you credibility, trust, and respect from the observer. Now it's time to let the observer know what made you start your brand. This has to be powerful and slightly dramatic to have the proper effect. It is supposed to strike an emotional chord with the observer and connect you to them in a manner that makes them take the plunge and decide that it is indeed you who they wish to make their tailor or custom clothier over and above others. Ours was as follows:

Once Ashish & Pawan had mastered the Drape Cut, they were asked by their master to spread their wings and raise awareness for the bespoke craft in a place where the knowledge of it was still nascent. Knights & Lords was formed in Dubai in 2010 to remind today's decision-makers of the importance of having gentlemanly attributes and preserving the traditions left behind by the nobles of yesteryear. It is for those who wish to preserve the supreme culture of being a true gentleman who, alongside doing justice to his true life purpose, also considers it his duty and responsibility to dress like who he wants to be.

Notice how the above starts with highlighting the one thing that made us decide on starting our own tailoring house. In our case, it was our master telling us that we had learned and mastered the Drape Cut and that we were ready to spread our wings. The next part states our brand philosophy of how we believe in the culture and tradition of being a gentleman and the importance of dressing, not like who you are but who you want to be. This firstly is targeted to inspire the observer to want to become a gentleman and, secondly, aspire towards dressing like the person he wishes to be in the future. A combination that is meant to inspire and aspire him towards choosing us as his custom clothier over and above others.

What is the motive behind it, and what you wish to accomplish with it?

This is the final part of your brand story. It is supposed to provide a closure to your story by showcasing that the true motive behind your business is contributing to a greater cause. It is important to make sure that this does not state any financial gain or personal success as reasons or motives behind your tailoring house. It is important to show your observer who has by now almost converted to being your client that you first and foremost have their benefit and the benefit of the community at large over and above anything else. This tells the observer that you are selfless and passionate about what you do and are not there to make money out of this entire arrangement. Your main focus is the satisfaction of your clients and contributing to the community and society at large.

Our motive in our brand story is as follows:

Ashish & Pawan wish to bring a wave in The New Bespoke Movement by making sure a Bespoke Suit is something that can be enjoyed by anyone and everyone and not something that is out of reach for the masses. They wish to see a world where everyone has opened their 'Eye of Bespoke.'

The above is a short closure to the brand story that tells the observer that we would like to see a world where everyone has and is able to experience bespoke clothing by giving the message that we are not there just to seek financial advancement but instead are priced reasonably as our main motive is to make sure as many people are able to experience bespoke craftsmanship as possible.

After your story is complete, you need to ensure that you project a brand image that illustrates success as this is a crucial step towards your business success. So make sure your brand image already shows that you are successful. People get attracted to positivity and success because that is what they aspire to be. Projecting that you are already a successful brand will make them feel that they should come to you because they believe they too are either already successful, or want to be successful and this thought of theirs aligns with your brand.

In order to have consistently sustained profits, you need to figure out ways to attract a more elite clientele. That's the only way to create sustainable success - especially during challenging times.

This is far easier than one can imagine and can be done by implementing three simple techniques. If you implement these consistently, it will be possible to attract this elite clientele more easily. It all starts with the law of attraction and skillful and intentional use of the ABCs (Appearance, Behavior, and Communication skills).

The law of attraction says that you attract into your life what you think about, dwell upon, get into action, or show to the world as you attempt to externally manifest your professional goals and passionate dreams to make them a reality. As the quote cited above says, "we attract what we are." That's why those who ARE very successful want to work with or attract professionals who look, behave, and communicate on the same level or higher than they do. They want to team up with those who enhance them, empower them, and make them feel better about themselves — which is why you have to present yourself as the type of professional who can bring all of that to the table through your unique value-adding talents and benefits. We all love to be around highly successful people who can help us launch our careers, stretch us up a notch, and give us that sensational experience of powerful synergy with a team player, partner, client, vendor, or employee who is really gifted, talented, and helpful.

Use Power Dressing Techniques

If you want to attract a more elite clientele, it's important that your overall image be top-notch. Why? Most highly successful, elite clients dress in a very powerful and commanding fashion. They have already learned the importance of silent messages conveyed by their dressing and grooming habits, and they strategically leverage them to project their image and brand. They want to surround themselves with the best team. It is a basic requirement for yourself to use the same power dressing techniques to be noticed and valued by these individuals.

When you meet with a client or potential client, they begin judging you from the moment they step through your door. They want the best person or the company with the strongest brand to give them the services that they need, and they will pay a premium to work with highly successful people who carry themselves with a powerful presence.

Confidence Magnetically Attracts Top-Tier Clients

People love working with those who are confident in their skills, abilities, and resources for solving problems with a results-oriented attitude. By the same token, nobody wants to work with a person or organization that lacks a self-assured and competent presence. Don't misunderstand – We are not talking about being overly confident in a way that borders on arrogance or belittles people. What we are talking about is authentic confidence that is conveyed naturally in your posture, your warm body language, the way you respect others, and your positive outlook.

When you are confident in your presence, you easily attract top-tier clients to want to be around you. But if you are sending mixed signals through your personal presence, you have to work that much harder to attract these same clients. When you exude confidence through your presence ABCs, you magnetically attract a similar type of person who is also highly successful and confident and can help you leverage your bespoke business.

Positive Vibes to Enhance Communication

Another facet of your image that will help to attract elite client is verbal communication. To resonate with this elite group, your communication has to have a positive vibration, the proper vernacular, and a style that matches theirs. Some professionals like to be presented with the bottom-line results, for example, so with those clients, you can provide a snapshot, quick summary, or a final cost. Others prefer to communicate about their personal lives and have you really get to know them as a person before getting down to discussing how you can solve their problem.

With those people, you may need to talk about your common interests and establish a friendly connection before you launch into a business conversation.

Higher-level clients also want to do business with people who pay in full and on time, trust them to solve their clothing challenges, and help them catapult their careers upward. When you upgrade your presence to a level that resonates with this rarefied demographic, you will be amazed at how you magnetically attract those top-tier clients to want to work with you. Like magic, they pre-qualify themselves out of their own desire to win you over. Because you create a successful presence that conveys that you are the best, in other words, the best clients gravitate towards you. Just practice these simple techniques, and you will begin to more easily attract a higher-level clientele for professional sustainability and business growth.

Now that your building your brand image and brand story is complete, the next step is to raise awareness for it so that as many potential clients notice it as possible. The right ones who feel that your brand story matches with their ideology will convert to being a client by getting in touch with you themselves.

RAISING AWARENESS

"Awareness is the greatest agent for change."
-Eckhart Tolle

As opposed to ready-made clothing, in the bespoke custom clothing industry, potential clients will never choose you over others simply because of your price. Price comes second to what they are looking for which is the perfect 'FIT.' The 'FIT' in this case is not just to do with the size of the clothing but the actual brand and the person behind it. The entire brand story and the philosophy behind it needs to fit in with their ideology and personality for them to choose you. For this reason, traditional marketing and advertising methods, which are mainly geared towards the four Ps (Product, Price, Promotion, Place), do not work.

These clients have gone through the entire journey of shopping in malls during special offers for ready-made clothing and are interested in coming to you simply because they have not been satisfied with their experience thus far and feel something is lacking, which you can fulfill. For this reason, just an ad in the paper or a magazine that tells them about the product at an attractive price for which they can get it with an attractive location where they can avail it will not make them take the plunge. You need to use creative ways to raise awareness about yourself using your brand story and other methods to create a memorable impression in their minds. This is to be done in a manner that focuses on those very aspects that they feel is lacking with other ready-made brands which are proper guidance, expertise, knowledge, and experience. You have to raise awareness of the fact that you can provide these by using the following methods:

Spreading your brand story across the media

Positioning yourself as an authority

Spreading knowledge

We have used the three methods mentioned above and it has worked well for us. However, raising awareness is not limited to just what has been stated above. It is suggested that once all the above methods are done in the order mentioned, you may add other methods to it. The specifics of how we executed each of the above methods are mentioned below.

Spreading your brand story across the media

Once we had established our brand story, we put it out to all the major relevant magazines, newspapers, and print media in the region. Our business, brand story, and interviews were featured in the following print media titles:

- The Rake Magazine

- Esquire Magazine

- Friday Magazine, Gulf News

- WKND Magazine, Khaleej Times

- CEO Magazine

- Gulf Business Magazine

- Arabian Business

- Signe Magazine

Once we were featured extensively in the titles mentioned above detailing our craft, the right kind of people started getting in touch with us themselves and easily converted to becoming our clients. They were exactly the kind of people we expected to have as clients since they had read everything about us and got in touch with us because they felt what we were offering was exactly what they were looking for. We put what we were doing out there, and the people who it appealed to reached out to us. From then on, the journey became easier as the word-of-mouth and client referrals started doing the work for us to get new clients through our door.

Positioning yourself as an authority

When we got in touch with Debonair magazine, they mentioned that they did not want to do a regular feature on us. Instead, they wanted us to pen a regular column in their magazine about bespoke craftsmanship and suit making as an authority on the topic in the region due to our credentials of being trained from the birthplace of bespoke tailoring, which is Savile Row in London. This was a new and welcomed avenue for us, and we started writing a monthly column in the Debonair Magazine called "Needle & Thread," which provided knowledge on bespoke tailoring, craftsmanship, and dressing etiquettes for the modern gentleman. Once these columns started getting noticed, we were approached by several other magazines to write similar columns for them such as WKND Magazine, Khaleej Times and Friday Magazine, Gulf News where observers were able to ask us sartorial questions which were answered by us in print for others to read as well.

This helped us to keep ourselves connected to the mass audience and be viewed as an authority and an expert in our field of work. People did not come to us for just a suit anymore. They came to us for the entire experience of getting the knowledge behind everything with regards to it and getting our expert advice on the right way to build their wardrobe in a manner that every piece in it was an investment that will serve its purpose for many years to come. We started receiving more specific requests for commissions for work wear and leisure wear. People wanted to take a deeper dive into investing in their wardrobe with us where every piece crafted by us served a specific purpose. It also increased our following largely since observers kept noticing us in different places and made us remain on the top of their minds whenever they needed any sartorial advice. We have so far written over 70 articles and continue to write columns for print and online magazines.

Spreading knowledge

After we had developed a decent enough following, we started spreading the knowledge that we had written about in person by conducting masterclasses and focusing on more speaking engagements. People were interested in getting more understanding and learning directly from us as they had been following us through reading our articles for some time now. Getting that very thing with us in person was something which not only did they enjoy, but also helped to reinforce in their minds that we were indeed the experts in our field of work. We were able to give practical knowledge by showcasing different aspects of dressing, such as different ways of tying a tie or different ways of folding a pocket square along with the purpose of each. It made them want to get a suit from us or a tie from us so that they can practice what they have learned and implement it in their daily life. This ensured that whenever they required a custom clothier, they would turn to us over and above anyone else due to the sartorial knowledge and understanding they had already gained from us. They were also more prone to speak about us to others whenever they engaged in sartorial talks or were complimented in a certain aspect of their dressing from their peers. They would make it known that they have learned this from our articles that they have read or our masterclasses that they have attended, which organically increased our following through word of mouth.

Opting to raise awareness in creative ways and shying away from the conventional advertising and marketing methods helped us greatly to build a consistent and robust base of loyal clients and followers while giving a boost to our public image and brand presence. We ended up having a customer retention rate of 98%, meaning a client who would commission a garment from us would return to us 98% of the time within six months. We credit our methods of raising awareness with not only getting the right clientele through our door but also with keeping our clients with us. It also helped attract the right kind of clientele towards us, some of whom have been notable figures, heads of state, and celebrities such as Mike Tyson, Luis Fonsi, Jay Sean, and Kelis, among others.

DO IT YOURSELF!

> *"If you want a thing done well,*
> *do it yourself."*
> *-Napoleon Bonaparte*

With our organic following and clientele that gradually but consistently kept increasing due to our techniques of raising awareness, we made sure we did as much as possible ourselves. Every client who would commission a bespoke garment of any kind would deal with us personally during which we would understand exactly what the purpose was for the garment being commissioned and the lifestyle preferences of our client after which we would carefully guide them through the entire process of selecting what would be best suited for them according to us. We would make sure we measure each client ourselves and then cut those commissions and supervise its crafting from scratch to finish.

This was done because we felt that it was important first to realize that these clients had reached our doorstep because they were looking for more than just a suit or a shirt. They were looking for advice from someone they considered an expert in the field of style. They wanted to invest and not spend on the garments in their wardrobe. They wanted advice on the right way to build their wardrobe with garments that matched their style and would become a signature statement of theirs while being in line with their lifestyle preferences. Above all, they were looking to have a memorable journey while accomplishing all of this, unlike being treated as a number by a salesperson at a store selling ready-made garments. This meant that having the personal touch of our faces being present at all times was a must. They needed to feel that they were embarking on their journey personally with us who were representing Knights & Lords and not just making a purchase from a brand, as is the case in a ready-made store.

All our clients appreciated that they could sit across and discuss everything about their commissions directly with us, the very same people who they had read about, and followed through our articles and presence in media. The very same individuals who were the face of Knights & Lords' tailoring house were the ones they were dealing with directly, and we gave them our attention by taking them through the entire journey of commissioning their garments ourselves. It was the same surreal feeling of watching a movie and then having the opportunity to interview the actor or the director to get further insight into the movie first hand from the people involved in it. They felt good that their garments were made not just to fit their bodies but who they are as individuals. Our clients furthermore felt privileged to know that the very same hands that measured and crafted the suits of notable figures, heads of state, and celebrities were the ones measuring and crafting their garments as well.

We even made sure we handled all the complementary aspects to our business ourselves, such as our social media channels, our website, and any other content that we used for communicating with our clients and followers. It didn't mean that we did everything perfectly, but we did it in a manner that was reflective of who we are. Our clients could immediately see, read, and have a sense that all of this indeed was done by us as it had the undertone of our personalities.

This furthermore gave Knights & Lords a personal and individualistic outlook as everything was in line with the people they eventually met and were running it. Our individuality needed to be showcased rather than the archetypal corporate brand that people typically see and expect in all channels: personal and online. After all, any business that is related to personalization and customization is meant to embrace the imperfections and use them to create an enhanced version of the image a person wishes to see with the same imperfections present as a stamp of its individuality.

We did exactly that by doing as much as we could ourselves without relying on any other professionals who could do the work for us, and it contributed immensely in creating a satisfactory interaction and a memorable journey for our clients. The advocacy from clients was much stronger since, at every stage, they had dealt with us right from choosing their threads to finally receiving the suit from our very hands. This helped in building a personal rapport with them that kept on being nurtured over all the years they placed their commissions with us.

NEVER SAY NO!

> *"Never say 'no' to adventures."*
> *-Ian Fleming*

When clients would come to us after reading about us, reading our articles on dressing etiquette for the modern gentleman, and knowing about the noteworthy and celebrity clientele that we had, it was only natural for them to expect that we could do almost anything that they could imagine. We made sure we kept up to that expectation. We tried our best to never say 'NO' to a request made by a client as long as it was within the realm of tailoring. We instead encouraged them to think out of the box and let us know what they would wish to have in their suits that are otherwise missing in their fashionable garments and made sure we incorporated it in their garments.

Every person has their individualistic taste and specific design requests owing to their pleasure or lifestyle and shouldn't be disregarded as being too trivial to be exercised, which either puts them in an awkward spot or feeling belittled the other way around. They should feel proud of their individuality, and their personality traits and their garments should psychologically reinforce the fact that they are one of a kind and special.

There is an instance when we had an Austrian gentleman requesting a specialized pocket in the interior of his about to be commissioned green blazer to fit his small pocket umbrella. While he kept asking us, if it is alright to accommodate his request, we wholeheartedly encouraged the same and asked him to give us his pocket umbrella for us to attempt making a pocket exacting to its measurements while making the construction of the jacket in a manner that the balance is maintained in the left and right side even after the umbrella is placed inside the pocket on one side. Towards the end, he was extremely pleased and said that he would never forget this blazer, and it was a prized addition to his wardrobe. We understood well that people like to be connected emotionally with things that they use, especially when it makes them feel it is something individual and personal to fulfil their exacting needs and desires. That is the true essence and purpose of getting something made especially for yourself and get the true feeling of having a garment that is custom-made as it has something that no one else had, personalized to a degree much deeper than only measurements but also in sync with your lifestyle preferences. That is what gives the feeling that this garment is yours and yours alone in its truest sense.

In another instance, we had a gentleman who wanted to commission a bespoke suit that would be a perfect representation of his prized automobile, which was a Maserati. Apart from the suit having his design preferences with his exacting measurements, it had to have the same design influences as his car to ultimately make the suit an extension of his lifestyle.

It began with having the suit in a particular black fabric that had to be the darkest possible tone to reflect on the diamond black tone of the car. This was achieved with a black all wool fabric that was dyed seven times to achieve that color to give it that distinguished look. The car had carbon-fiber interior accents, and this aspect was reflected by having a custom-designed lining of that print inside the bespoke suit creation. Other details like the canary yellow, black stitching done on the interior seats of the car were reflected with the yellow piping detailing and the monogramming of his initials done in that font color on the inside of the suit jacket. But this is not where it all ended. The Maserati has a very distinguishable logo in the form of a trident, and the challenge was to have that aspect being interpreted in the suit jacket as well. We ultimately came up with the idea of having the chest pocket of the suit jacket cut in the three-pronged trident shape. Since in a car, the symbol is the first most identifiable decoration, the particular emphasis would also be placed on the chest pocket with the gentlemen always placing a pocket square that would draw attention there with people noticing the three-pronged design of the pocket on the suit jacket.

With this suit commission, the gentleman felt like leaving a design signature that would be identifiable by others who would have a keen eye and attention to detail. It would also showcase his mature sartorial understanding of crafts to make creative decisions that became an extension of his identity. It furthermore showcased his passion for automobiles and showed the observer that he took great pride in his most prized possession, which was his Maserati car. This gentleman eventually ended up becoming the President of the Maserati owners club, which had hundreds of members who regarded him as the ultimate Maserati connoisseur.

Accommodating all the requests made by clients not only helped us win them as a client for life but also taught us a lot about the different tastes, interests, and personal preferences of individuals that we built on and began offering to almost everyone intuitively. During every initial drafting session as soon as we would get a glimpse of their inner personality, we would offer and suggest something to be done within the garments commissioned that would be relevant and in line with their personality without them having to ask for it. This took our customer interaction with service levels and client experience to a whole new level, which they knew they could not expect anywhere else.

PROVIDE INTUITIVE CUSTOMER SERVICE

"The intuitive mind is a sacred gift, and the rational mind is a faithful servant. We have created a society that honors the servant and has forgotten the gift."
-Albert Einstein

Providing intuitive customer service is about developing a sense of knowing the things that are not seen or are immediately apparent, neither to yourself nor to the client. To sense these things which they desire deep down and provide exactly that without the client having to ask for it is the only way to open the door for your clients to experience the delight of unknown pleasures.

A perfect example of this was when we had a gentleman commissioning a suit who kept excusing himself for a break every ten minutes. With our initial drafting session, which usually lasts ninety minutes, this was quite a few breaks that he kept talking about and was hence making the session a lot longer than usual. Upon inquiring why, he kept taking these short breaks, he mentioned that he was a chronic smoker who usually smoked close to two packs a day. He further expressed how frustrated he was of this "problem" of having to excuse himself now and then for a smoke regardless of whether he was in the midst of an important meeting or at dinner with someone or even while going to the movies with his family. He felt this was not just taking a toll on his health but also on his general way of life. He also joked about how even a well-tailored suit could not help because his trouser pockets would always bulge with the packs of cigarettes he carried around. Once his session was done, we sat down and started brainstorming what we can do with this information. Here was a client who had a genuine problem that we found out, which was affecting his health and his life in general. More importantly, he expressed that he was frustrated with it and wished something could be done about it. Though he did not ask us to do something about it or to help him in any way, we knew as people; we had to show empathy and address this in any way we can. He furthermore expressed a dislike towards cigarette packs making his trouser pockets bulge. This helped us come up with an idea.

We created individual slits inside his jacket pocket. Each slit was exacting to the measurement of a cigarette with a small elastic band on top made in a manner that the cigarettes would not topple over each other. We, however, made only five slits inside, hoping that a day would come when he would reduce his intake to just five cigarettes a day. We did this without letting him know and called him in for his first fitting. When he came in for the fitting and learned of this innovation we had done to his suit, he was ecstatic and gave us his limited edition Zippo lighter to make a pocket next to it, exacting to the measurements of his lighter. His ecstatic state turned confused when he discovered that there were only five slits. We mentioned that this was done intentionally as a motivation to curb his smoking habit and if he was not successful, we could add more slits later on.

He received his suits after all the fittings were done and returned to us after two months to commission a couple of shirts. We asked how the suit we had crafted was serving him, and to our surprise, he had reduced his smoking from roughly two packs of cigarettes in a day to just five cigarettes a day. He mentioned now that he had such a well-cut and well-fitted suit; he did not want to spoil the look by carrying big packs of cigarettes in his trouser pockets. Moreover, he felt embarrassed to ask us for more slits, which would make him feel that he had somehow lost the challenge of being able to curb his smoking. He felt what we had done was great and done with the right intention, which gave him the push to try and curb his smoking habit. It was now or never, and now that he was successful at doing it, he wanted to return to us to commission a few shirts to reward himself and share his story of success with us.

The above things made it clear to us that there are three key aspects to providing intuitive customer service:

Analyzing your interaction with your client

We analyzed our interaction and sensed that our client needed a solution to his smoking habit.

Doing something special for the client out of empathy

We felt the need to do something now that we knew about this habit that was proving to be a problem for our client.

Innovate in a manner that inspires the client to become a better version of themselves

We innovated with adding cigarette slits inside his jacket in a manner that gave him the motivation to curb his habit by providing only five slits inside his jacket and aspire towards eventually reducing his smoking to just five cigarettes a day.

By using the three aspects of providing intuitive customer service, we were able to reach a customer retention rate of 98%, which means that a client who would visit us would come back to us 98% of the time within six months. This was only because they started feeling that the garments we created could do more than make them look good. They felt that it could create a deep dimensional shift within their inner being and could make them a better version of themselves. This was solely credited to providing intuitive customer service, which was attaining something they otherwise did not expect. This further reinforced in their mind that it was something they could only expect or rather hope for only with us at Knights & Lords and no other tailoring house.

Moreover, showing empathy towards them gave a humane aspect to our relationship, with us now being considered as more than just their tailors. We were not only catering to their tailoring needs but also their emotional needs alongside it benefiting from ROE (Return on Empathy). The importance of benefiting from ROE is best described in the book written by Gaurav Sinha called "Compassion INC.," which is a recommended read for everyone who wishes to understand the concept of using empathy. It is a book that inspired us greatly to perfect the intuitive customer service strategy with empathy being a major part of it and getting the most from ROE.

STRETCH
THE LIMITS!

"One finds limits by pushing them."
-Herbert Simon

After accommodating all requests of clients and not saying 'No' to even the most extraordinary requests by clients, we were pushed to the next step in our craft. Clients wanted to place their commissions with the intention of pushing the limits of bespoke. This coupled with providing intuitive customer service whereby we sensed what the client would wish for and incorporating it into the suit without them having to ask added another dimension to our practice of the craft. These clients didn't go through the routine of choosing fabrics, talking about the style, and so on. Conversations with them were more abstract, and the challenge was to reach into the farthest depths of their imagination and bring forth that image they had of themselves through just this abstract conversation.

One such client who was an important head of state wanted to commission a suit which, when he walked into a room, would tell others who he was without him having to utter a word or be introduced by anyone. This was the only brief we got, and he said we might charge whatever price we like for the suit as long as this was achieved. It was barely a five-minute conversation with the pressure on us to deliver what he wanted. We knew when there is so little known, the best place to start is to get to know more about the person. We did some research on his background and his preferences when it came to dressing in suits and found out that it was always conservative, classic, and subtle pinstripes. We knew anything we did on the details or the style of the suit would not be sufficient as when he would walk in the room, people would take notice of him but not necessarily know who he is. Since his style was classic and subtle, we had to convey who he was subtly. We thought of a suit that had subtle pinstripes when seen from far, but when given a closer look would reveal that the pinstripes are his name written in a tiny font from top to bottom in a repeated manner. This way, whenever he walks into the room, people would certainly know who he is without him having to speak a word and definitely without needing any introduction.

We spoke to our mill and toyed with the idea of creating a single length of fabric enough for one suit, especially for him, with his name woven within the fabric as pinstripes, which was possible. There was a bit of back and forth on the exact size of the font and spacing between the stripes, but the fabric finally got woven and came to us. It had the perfect balance of subtlety with fine pinstripes in the letters spelling out only when viewed at close proximity. We began crafting the suit, which took three months simply because the name needed to have a continuation and could not be broken anywhere, which meant that it needed to spell out and continue letter by letter all through the pockets and even through the belt loops in the trouser. Finally, the suit was crafted with precision and perfection, and when worn by our client, the feeling was too sublime to express it in words. He said that we had done it and pulled out his credit card and handed it to us to charge what we like.

This experience opened up our understanding to a new level whereby we began offering a service called "beyond bespoke' whereby everything could be made especially for the client such as the suit fabric, the lining, the buttons, a certain thread color to be used for the buttonholes and anything else. We started getting clients who would like a suit to be the same color as their Rolls-Royce cars or be an exact representation of his wife or girlfriends' Birkin bag, which stretched the limits of bespoke craftsmanship and our imagination with it.

What we learned as part of this was the fact that if you make something that people can only imagine, it helps them to believe that anything is possible once they wear it subconsciously. It keeps giving their mind the message that if the suit that they are wearing is likely to make, then achieving anything while wearing it is also possible. This was a priceless feeling, and they would offer willingly to pay any price for a garment or any item that stretched the limits of bespoke craftsmanship. It opened up our clientele to people who were used to having everything right from their garments to their shoes including their hats or their pens or anything they used specially made for them. This was done simply because each item reinforced in their mind that if this is possible, then anything is. This, however puts them in a mental state that allowed them to reach their full potential while making us a channel through which they could reach that state of mind.

People seeking excellence is one of the reasons for commissioning a bespoke garment for it to act as an anchor for them to perform at their best potential. On other occasions, if they already excel in their line of work, they would like to celebrate that and adopt that excellence with everything they do. And they would like to be invested in, by extension, in bespoke garments they would wear, leaving their mark or lifestyle signature on those as well. They then like to seek creative individuals who can translate their vision into items they would like to possess. It is the same line of thought as someone wanting to commission a painting or an art installation as is with bespoke clothing but can be more approachable than the former.

There is a separate feeling of personal joy when one has accomplished a new feat or something unique or innovative. This same feeling is extended when one successfully can commission something not done before and just a thought or a figment of their imagination that has been brought to reality through craftsmanship. That feeling is purely surreal.

THE EXPERIENCE BOOK

"The purpose of life is to live it, to taste experience to the utmost, to reach out eagerly and without fear for a newer and richer experience."
- Eleanor Roosevelt

The experience of a person while acquiring a premium product, commissioning a bespoke service, is shaped by the interaction during the entire process from start to finish along with the product or service being of immaculate quality and as per their preferences. The journey of acquiring the product or enjoying a service is as important as the actual product or the service itself. Various touchpoints can characterize the entire journey throughout the experience.

The first touchpoint is how they found out about the product or the service.

-Was it noticing it in popular or niche media in print or online media, either via articles or advertisements?

-Was it by a referral from a family member or friend who has been an existing user of the service or product?

- Is it affirmed by someone you admire, appreciate their persona, who could be a celebrity or a fairly visible social personality?

The second touch point would be the approach to the brand/service provider.

-Is it communicative with the following decorum either by phone or email?

Ability to answer queries or clarifications and ensuring the person requesting it is satisfied with the responses, with the queries being properly addressed.

The third touchpoint is personal interaction when they would like to avail of the product or service.

-Was enough expert assistance or guidance provided to ensure that a decision could be taken?

-Was the interaction at a comfortable pace without the feeling of being rushed or strong eagerness to close the transaction as soon as possible?

The fourth touchpoint is the comfort, attention to detail provided during the entire process of acquiring the product.

The fifth touchpoint is the actual product and service at the time it is acquired. This should speak of the quality and immaculate craftsmanship, which is the result of the previous interactions and the previous four touchpoints.

The sixth and final touchpoint is if they can mention or voice their journey during the entire process of acquiring the product or the service.

-Is this going to be in person or done online?

Now, people can voice their experience publicly using online mediums like Google reviews. It is usually noted that people are more prompt to mention a negative experience than a regular good experience. It takes a truly wonderful experience for them to publicly mention a positive review of the experience with a product or service. Sometimes people are also not that communicative in person to voice their experience and may pen their experience if they didn't feel they got an apt opportunity to mention it or were not asked by the service provider or the brand.

It is important to be communicative with the client and ensuring that you know how they feel about your product or service at the time of them receiving or acquiring it. A great way to do so is to have the 'Book of Experience.' Our 'Book of Experience' has a handmade wool cover with buttons sewn on it to showcase our bespoke craftsmanship. We developed this tradition of every individual who experienced a bespoke garment from Knights & Lords to pen down their experience at the time of finally receiving it from us.

Firstly, in this day and age of computers and smartphones, where the written word is done digitally rather than manually, this comes as a welcome surprise. It also reflects on the culture and the old tradition of the written word and reinforces the age-old saying, 'The pen is mightier than the sword.'

People take a moment to think before they start penning their thoughts. They also usually like to read what others before them have written. This makes them realize that others after them may read what they have written, and hence subconsciously, it puts the responsibility on them to be as honest as they can. They may also have the last hand written note from something years back in university or even in school. This activity in itself hence becomes a memorable experience as they are reliving it. Additionally, it also reinforces in their mind what they write, and they become more conscious of their experience and immensely helps in building loyalty and customer retention among clients. Furthermore, it tells you exactly what they think as most people are usually not able to verbalize it effectively.

A great experience gives positivity to the person about the product or service. Writing about it makes them more mindfully aware of it, and they will continually want to come and experience the product and service from you for years to come to re-live the entire journey they have had with you.

MENTORING

*"A mentor is someone who allows you to see
the higher part of yourself when sometimes
it becomes hidden to your view."
- Oprah Winfrey*

We had explored almost everything there was in terms of making our craft better and providing clients with more than what they could imagine with the garments they had commissioned with us. We learned that throughout the journey of commissioning bespoke garments with us, our clients began to gain a deeper understanding of themselves, their personalities, and their desires, making them want to explore deeper into the areas of their innate passion and deeper dimensions. They came to us to seek knowledge of different forms of craftsmanship to discover where their interests and passions lie. This made us mentor them in that particular realm which they desired to become a master of.

Mentoring meant making them aware of the different realms of craftsmanship that exist so they can find ones that appeal to them, such as bespoke garments, shoes, cigars, single malts, watches, and any such products or services that involved a traditional craft done by hand. After they had discovered which ones appealed to them, we would get them started by guiding them on the first steps towards gaining the knowledge of how these finely crafted items were brought into existence to take a deep dive into the story of their creation. Seeing and understanding these items from the eyes of the creator is what makes one appreciate the craft behind it. It is only then that one can take the true pleasure from appreciating and indulging themselves in the craft of the item or service that is used or consumed.

Soon we began to see that clients who we were mentoring slowly became collectors and connoisseurs of the products or services that appealed to them. Being seen as collectors and connoisseurs gave them a certain kind of respect in their circles, which helped them immensely to become recognized figures in their community. Being recognized figures helped them professionally as well as now they have known figures who could easily connect with others over common interests shared between themselves. Their knowledge and passion gave others the message that whatever they do, they do it well, an elevated image projection that contributed to their success.

Due to this and the maturity in their understanding of craftsmanship that they gained with us mentoring them, they began to appreciate what we do even more, and they became strong advocates of our philosophy and our craft. With time, we began to see a growing community of advocates of Knights & Lords who were also connoisseurs or collectors of other things with a significant following of their own. We understood that the next step would be formally acknowledging this community of advocates that we had so they could further spread the awareness of our craft.

BUILDING A COMMUNITY OF ADVOCATES

"Victory in marketing doesn't happen when you sell something, but when you cultivate advocates for your brand."
-Steve Knox

The community of advocates that we built through mentoring had to be formalized so that they could feel a sense of belonging towards Knights & Lords.

This would consist of the following:

- Establishing the name of this group to have it formalized.

- Establishing the criteria and the requirements of being part of this group.

- Giving them a physical item that identifies them as a member of this group.

- The benefits and privileges they could avail of if they are a part of this group.

Establishing the name of this group

Unlike common beliefs, this is supposed to be the simplest part of the formalization process. The name is supposed to be as simple as possible so that it easily sticks to one's head. For that to happen; it should be no longer than three words since historically, the most successful societies, groups or private member's clubs had simple names that consisted of three words or lesser. The name should also be something that should be able to encompass almost everything under its umbrella to not risk having to change it in the future, should the opportunity arise to expand its reach to different realms and avenues. We settled for "Knights & Lords Elite Club" as it was simple, sophisticated, relevant, and easy to remember.

Establishing the criteria and the requirements of being part of this group

The reason for the whole formalization process to start with was because of the community of advocates that we had, so by default, being an advocate of Knights & Lords was the first criteria. We also had to ensure that being eligible should have an aspirational value to it, and we noticed that most of our advocates had a certain spend pattern. They were all spending between AED 20,000 to AED 50,000 in a year at Knights & Lords. We hence decided to keep one of the criteria as having a minimum spend of AED 25,000 and up. This made everyone we were mentoring, aspire towards reaching that slightly higher spend bracket on becoming eligible for membership to the Knights & Lords Elite Club, which helped us to increase our revenues due to this aspirational aspect in our criteria.

Giving them a physical item that identifies them as a member of this group

The first thing that comes to mind in this area is membership cards. We, however, wanted to make them slightly different that appeared more coveted, premium, and elite. Instead of regular membership cards, we decided to make credit cards that were metallic with Knights & Lords Elite Club mentioned along with our logo laser engraved on the credit card. We also further personalized each card with the member's name engraved on it. This made the members use their card wherever they would like to pay in a group of people when they wanted to show that they were members of an elite club. Noticing this made others curious enough to ask about the cards and about how to become members making it easier for our advocates, who were now even members of our elite club to spread awareness about us. We made the cards in three different finishes: black, silver and gold. This was then given to our members based on their annual spend with us. This again made members who had the black or silver aspire towards the gold card and made the gold card members present it with pride wherever they could, which further increased our branding and awareness within the respective micro-communities of our members.

The benefits and privileges they could avail of if they are a part of this group

We made sure that all Knights & Lords Elite Club members were well taken care of and saw value in being and remaining members, by providing them with special benefits and privileges. We knew that they were all like-minded people who would love to mingle with each other, so the first thing we did was give each of them access to the entire roster of members to be able to network with another fellow member. We also made introductions between them upon special request if any one of them wanted to connect with another specific member for any reason. We furthermore started holding special events based on craftsmanship, which all our members could attend to witness different forms of craftsmanship and exchange knowledge with each other while they are taking a deep dive into it. We would partner with different brands and allow them to showcase their craft to our members and explain the history and heritage of their brand along with giving a glimpse of behind-the-scenes of what goes into crafting their products. Slowly, we accumulated a significant number of these partners who would take part in our events, and we decided to get them involved in our membership by allowing them to provide some form of lifestyle benefits to our members. This helped to promote them within our membership database and gave our members extra added benefits for being members of the Knights & Lords Elite Club.

This network of advocates kept increasing as now these members who were also connoisseurs of some product or service had gained enough knowledge of the finer things in life and were mentoring others in their community. This was making these people mentored by our club members ready to become new members of our club eventually. Our club membership began to grow organically, where each member was managing and working hand-in-hand with one another to mentor and induct new members into the club.

GIVE SPECIAL TREATMENT TO ADVOCATES

"The best advertising you can have is a loyal customer spreading the word about how incredible your business is."
-Shep Hyken

The Knights & Lords Elite Club members, a community that was organically grown without any intervention or effort needed from our side, was our true wealth. We had to give back to the members by giving them priviledged assistance and benefits over and above other clients. We also wanted to ensure that this club was self-managed without us having to manage activities and experiences for them from time to time. We felt that a physical location where they could indulge in their practice of pleasure from time to time would help in making them feel special.

We got in touch with a cigar lounge in Fairmont - The Palm called "The Cigar Room," which we frequently visited and have our initial client sessions sometimes. We spoke to them about re-creating the Knights & Lords experience within The Cigar Room, where we could have our members come in to see and speak of commissions or to indulge and experience the finer things in life that they were accustomed to as connoisseurs. The Cigar Room welcomed this idea with open arms but wanted to re-create the experience in a manner that would be a world's first in terms of a journey into the depths of the different forms of craftsmanship and a celebration of craftsmanship.

This led us to get in touch with the world's finest single malt brand, "The Macallan," who we were strong advocates of bespoke craftsmanship right from the time when we were working on The Row in London. This idea quickly escalated into a collaborative partnership between The Macallan, The Cigar Room in Fairmont - The Palm, and us (Knights & Lords), resulting in "The Finest Cut." The Finest Cut, launched in 2019, was an exclusive purpose-built section within The Cigar Room made to celebrate the spirit of craftsmanship by drawing strong parallels between the craftsmanship of The Macallan, Knights & Lords and the various offerings of The Cigar Room. The finest single malts of The Macallan could now be enjoyed with the finest offerings of The Cigar Room while engaging in a discussion about their bespoke commissions from Knights & Lords in a uniquely designed relaxed area crafted to distinction. It also was a place where members could also mentor other potential members and perfect their practice of pleasure as connoisseurs.

The Finest Cut Lounge made our entire system of recruiting new members while making our existing ones feel special, completely self-managed with requiring very little involvement from our side. Moreover, people could now speak of commissioning garments over a drink or a cigar, which was an experience that they couldn't otherwise get with any other bespoke tailor or even any other retail vendor or service for that matter. Moreover, it gave the right kind of ambience and sense of belonging to our existing members while mentoring others. Finally, it was a perfect place for us to host events around craftsmanship, making every event that we would hold very special and memorable. Our member base now kept growing exponentially with us having to do very little for it since everything was being done at and by The Finest Cut.

KEEP GIVING MORE THAN A CUSTOM GARMENT

"Always deliver more than expected."
- Larry Page

Having 'The Finest Cut' working by our side and seeing our member base grow made us realize the importance of giving more than just a custom garment. People now came to commission bespoke garments from Knights & Lords because along with a custom garment came the following benefits:

- Access to "The Finest Cut Lounge"

- Introduction to the community of Elite Members.

- Being eligible to be mentored by an influential connoisseur and potentially becoming a member yourself.

- Gaining knowledge of the different forms of craftsmanship and becoming a connoisseur eventually.

- Becoming a known figure within the Elite Club and being connected to influential connoisseurs.

- Attending Knights & Lords events and connecting with the community at large as an individual personality and a recognized figure.

With being a client of Knights & Lords came an entire lifestyle that is meant to be lived by a true gentleman, along with being connected to a community of gentlemen who practices and lives it constantly. They also got the opportunity to learn and gain knowledge of things they never knew before, which would make them stand apart in the company of others, making them more influential in their micro-communities. They would be regarded as elite, and they were proud of it. They would commission just a bespoke garment, but what came as a package was much more than just a bespoke garment, and that is what gave Knights & Lords the continued customer retention compared to other tailoring houses.

In a competitive market where every other tailoring house would try to attract clients by giving better prices, Knights & Lords did not succumb to the price war and still managed to have a high customer retention due to all the added benefits that came with being a client of Knights & Lords which were basically standing on three pillars:

The Knights & Lords Elite Club

The ever-growing base of members who were also advocates

The Finest Cut

Using these three pillars properly put us in a place that allowed us to carve a space for ourselves that is unaffected by market conditions and helped us to have a constant and consistent growth. This was completely organic and didn't require us to spend on expensive marketing, advertising or branding exercises. It put us in a place that was above other tailoring houses and ensured that a client of Knights & Lords would always remain a client of Knights & Lords. They would want to keep enjoying the benefits that came with it and remain a part of the growing community of Elite Members.

Giving more than your promised product or service is a simple yet powerful strategy that we feel all businesses should adopt. This is what will give your respective business its individuality and differentiate the entity from others in the market offering similar products and services. Above all, it is the only thing that will ensure a long lasting client-vendor relationship that cannot be broken by other vendors ensuring the highest customer retention rate even if the market is price sensitive. Finally, it is the only strategy that will keep your business recession proof regardless of market conditions. Competing businesses with strategies on reduced pricing, promotions or any other factors would not affect your business, since people have gotten used to the lifestyle built around your product or service, benefits of which would help them personally and professionally. This will always make them maintain the relationship with your business, as it is not a luxury anymore but rather a priority in their life. The would need to budget for from the beginning of the year just like every other basic expense of theirs. This powerful strategy that is used by very few puts your business in a comfortable spot above everyone else in the market, a spot which can't be bought by many other more expensive strategies and is hence worth every bit of effort put into it.

CONCLUSION

We hope that reading this book not only adds value to you as a reader, craftsman or business person but will also addresses the business problems you might have or currently have with running your custom clothing business. It is, however, important that you don't leave any stone unturned and follow the right strategies to achieve business success.

We share the story of our journey with you with excitement to see you succeed in your business journey. We hope that you go through your business journey with patience knowing that success really is just around the corner. We believe that if you surround yourself with people who can complement your skills and expertise it will be much easier to reach where you truly belong. You run your business; your business shouldn't run you and so we hope you never blame your business for not being able to accomplish things and take responsibility. You need to be prepared to go beyond sewing custom garments or beyond just practising your craft and also put your mind to implementing business techniques that are out of the box which we have mentioned in this book. Once you successfully do that, there is no limit to what you can achieve with your custom business!

NOTES

www.ingramcontent.com/pod-product-compliance
Lightning Source LLC
Chambersburg PA
CBHW070544160726
48003CB00005B/1889